★★
★The Library of
American Landmarks™

THE VIETNAM VETERANS MEMORIAL

Patra McSharry Sevastiades

The Rosen Publishing Group's
PowerKids Press™
New York

Published in 1997 by The Rosen Publishing Group, Inc.
29 East 21st Street, New York, NY 10010

First Edition

Book Design: Danielle Primiceri

Photo Credits: Cover Peter Gridley/FPG International; pp. 4, 8–9, 11, 17 (inset) Archive Photos; p. 7 © Joe Viesti/Viesti Associates; p. 11 © Peter L. Gould/FPG International; p. 13 © Tom Wilson/FPG International; p. 14 © Ken Frick/International Stock; p. 18 © Mark Bolster/International Stock; p. 20 © Dan Coleman/FPG International.

Sevastiades, Patra McSharry.
   The Vietnam veterans memorial / Patra McSharry Sevastiades.
      p. cm. — (The Library of American landmarks)
   Includes index.
   Summary: Examines the history, purpose, design, and impact of the Vietnam Veterans Memorial.
   ISBN 0-8239-5019-0
   1. Vietnam Veterans Memorial (Washington, D.C.)—Juvenile literature. [1. Vietnam Veterans Memorial (Washington, D.C.). 2. National monuments.] I. Title. II. Series.
   DS559.83.W18S49 1997
   975.3—dc21
                                       97-10839
                                         CIP
                                       AC

Table of Contents

What Is a Memorial?

A **memorial** (mem-OR-ee-ul) is something that helps people remember a person or event. Memorials honor the people they help us to remember. Some memorials are **ceremonies** (SER-eh-mohn-eez). Others are **monuments** (MON-yoo-ments).

Many famous memorials were built in Washington, DC, the capital of the United States. One of them is the Vietnam Veterans Memorial. Most people know it simply as "the Wall."

Between 4 and 5 million people visit "the Wall" every year.

The Vietnam Veterans Memorial

The idea to build a memorial for the **veterans** (VET-er-inz) of the Vietnam War was suggested in 1979 by a man named Jan C. Scruggs. Jan was a soldier who had fought in the Vietnam War. He believed that the **sacrifice** (SAK-rih-fys) of thousands of American veterans had not been **honored** (ON-erd) by the American people.

Many Americans did not support the war in Vietnam. Jan understood this. He worried that the soldiers who fought there might be forgotten.

The names of all the veterans who died or are missing are shown on the walls of the ▶ Vietnam Veterans Memorial.

BERT MOORE Jr · ALBERT E PARR

JOHN J ADDUCI · HENRY G ALLE

BARRY J BEDARD · EARL C BROW

ARD B COMER Jr · ROBERT F CON

P A DUNCAN · CHARLES R FELLEN

OSEPH E HARDY · JOSEPH R HARR

N D PERKINS · BURTON K PHILIPS

B WH   H WHITTINGTO

CORMI   NA   OND K DISMU

L R LAVEZ   OBERT J NA

ACK W P   JERRY

MARVIN A V

WARD T DAVIS J

CHINA

VIETNAM

HANOI

MYANMAR

LAOS

THAILAND

CAMBODIA

SOUTH
CHINA SEA

ANDAMAN
SEA

The Vietnam War

The United States was involved in the Vietnam War from the 1950s until 1975. North Vietnam was **Communist** (KOM-yoo-nist). South Vietnam was not Communist. They fought against each other. The United States didn't want Communist ideas to spread. It helped South Vietnam fight North Vietnam for much of the war. In the 1960s, American men between the ages of 18 and 22 had to **register** (REH-jis-ter) for the **draft** (DRAFT). Many were chosen to become soldiers and were sent to Vietnam to fight.

◀ The Vietnam War lasted much longer than anyone thought it would.

Disagreeing About the War

Many Americans agreed that soldiers should fight in Vietnam. But as the years passed, some Americans began to disagree. The war had lasted for many years. Many Americans had been killed. And, despite American support, South Vietnam had been unable to defeat North Vietnam. Many Americans began to **protest** (PRO-test) the war. Some young men who were old enough to register for the draft refused to register. In 1969, almost 550,000 American soldiers were fighting in Vietnam.

Many people joined the peace movement, which taught that all war was wrong. ▶

Coming Home

In 1973, the United States government agreed to stop fighting in Vietnam. American soldiers came home. Many had seen their friends killed in battle. Others had lost an arm or a leg while fighting. Many had been captured by the North Vietnamese during the war.

But the American soldiers came home to find that many Americans did not support the war or anyone who was a part of it. Instead of feeling welcome, many veterans felt **unappreciated** (un-uh-PREE-she-ay-ted).

Many years after the Vietnam veterans returned from the war, their efforts were appreciated. ▶

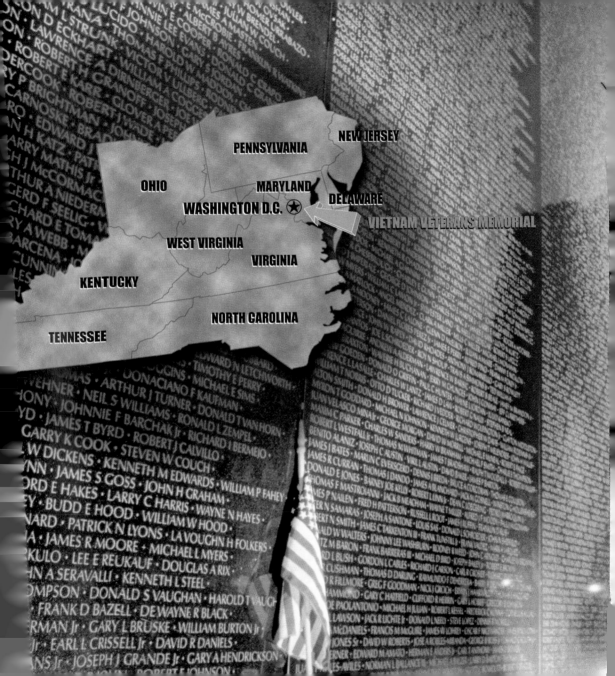

The Idea of a Memorial

In 1979, Jan Scruggs started to find support for the idea of building a memorial for the Vietnam veterans. He believed that:

- the name of every American soldier who had died during the war or was missing should appear on the memorial;
- the memorial should not tell people what to think about the Vietnam War;
- all of the money to pay for the memorial should come from people, not from the government;
- the memorial should be in Washington, DC.

◀ Jan Scruggs wanted the memorial to list every American soldier who died or disappeared in Vietnam.

Planning the Memorial

Many people liked Jan's idea for the memorial. Jan set up a **committee** (kuh-MIT-ee). The committee asked the U.S. Congress for land in Washington, DC, for a Vietnam veterans memorial. Congress agreed.

In 1981, the committee asked people to send them designs for the memorial. They received thousands of designs. The committee asked several artists to choose a design. After looking through all of them, the judges chose a design by a 21-year-old college student, Maya Ying Lin.

Maya Ying Lin was one of thousands of people ▶ who submitted designs for the memorial.

The Design

Maya's design was simple and beautiful. Two black **granite** (GRA-nit) walls, each about 247 feet long, met at an angle. Both walls were about ten feet tall at their highest points. The walls were polished until they reflected the sky, the ground, and the people who visited the memorial. The names of the 58,132 Vietnam veterans who had died or were missing were **etched** (ECHT) on the walls. The names are listed by the year each person died or disappeared.

◀ People come from all over the United States to find the names of loved ones, mourn the loss of friends, and see the memorial.

More Disagreements

Many people disagreed about the design of the memorial. Some thought Maya's design was ugly and did not honor the veterans. But many others agreed that it was a powerful memorial. At times, it seemed that the memorial would not be built because the design, like the war itself, was **controversial** (kon-tro-VER-shul). In the end, a bronze statue of three soldiers and a flagpole with an American flag were added. With these changes, Maya's design was finally accepted.

◀ Many people believe that the statue of the three soldiers completes the Vietnam Veterans Memorial.

The Memorial Is Finished

Jan collected $7 million in **donations** (doh-NAY-shunz) to pay for the memorial. In 1982, the memorial was finished. It was **dedicated** (DED-ih-kay-ted) on Veterans Day, November 11, 1982.

Six months later, in May 1983, President Ronald Reagan visited the memorial. As the commander-in-chief of all of the American Armed Forces, he gave the veterans the **recognition** (reh-kug-NISH-un) they had wanted and deserved for so long.

The sacrifice of the Vietnam veterans had finally been honored.

Glossary

ceremony (SER-eh-mohn-ee) A celebration in honor of something or someone.

committee (kuh-MIT-ee) A group of people that works together.

Communist (KOM-yoo-nist) A person who believes in a form of government in which everything is owned by the government and shared equally with all the people.

controversial (kon-tro-VER-shul) Causing disagreement.

dedicate (DED-ih-kayt) To set apart for a special reason.

donation (doh-NAY-shun) A gift, usually of money.

draft (DRAFT) The government selection of men to serve as soldiers.

etch (ECH) To cut an image into stone by using acid or other means.

granite (GRA-nit) A type of hard rock.

honor (ON-er) To show admiration for someone.

memorial (mem-OR-ee-ul) Something that reminds people of an important person or event.

monument (MON-yoo-ment) Something that is built to honor an important person or event.

protest (PRO-test) To speak out against something.

recognition (reh-kug-NISH-un) Official approval.

register (REH-jis-ter) To sign up for something.

sacrifice (SAK-rih-fys) The loss of something for the sake of something greater.

unappreciated (un-uh-PREE-she-ay-ted) Not valued.

veteran (VET-er-in) A soldier who has fought in a war.

Index